AL  on 12/14/1819 it became the 22nd state

"We Dare to Defend Our Rights"

The Yellowhammer State

Alabama

Montgomery

Camellia

Yellowhammer

Long Leaf Pine

Monarch butterfly

Blue Quartz

AK

Alaska
Juneau

on 1/3/1959 it became the 49th state

"North to the Future"

The Great Land

Forget Me Not

Sitka Spruce

Willow Ptarmigan

Skimmer Dragonfly

Gold

Jade

Iditarod

20 hours of sunlight

AZ

Arizona

on 2/14/1912 it became the 48th state

"God Enriches"

The Grand Canyon State

Phoenix ★

Yellow Palo Verde

Tree Frog

The Grand Canyon

Saguaro Cactus

Cactus Wren

Ringtail

Turquoise

Bolo Tie

AR

on 6/15/1836 it became the 25th state

"The People Rule"

The Natural State

Arkansas
Little Rock

- Loblolly Pine 
- Honeybee
- Apple Blossom
- Quartz crystal
- Mockingbird

CA

on 9/9/1850 it became the 31st state

California

"Eureka!"

Sacramento

The Golden State

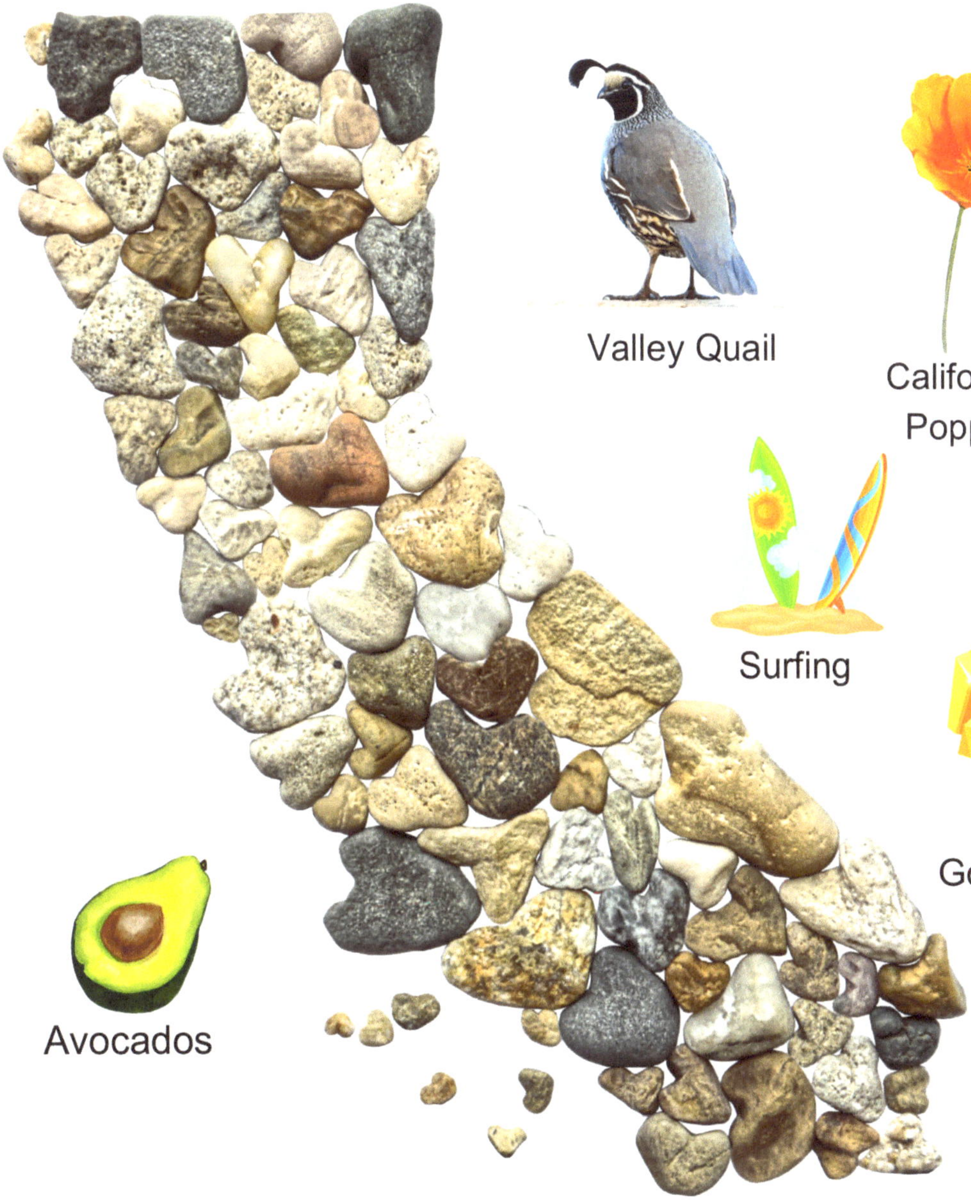

California Redwood

Grizzly Bear

Hollywood

Avocados

Valley Quail

California Poppy

Surfing

1848 Gold Rush

CO Colorado

Denver

on 8/1/1876 it became the 38th state

"Nothing without Provence"

The Centennial State

Rocky Mountain Columbine

Rocky Mountain Big Horned Sheep

Western painted Turtle

Lark Bunting

Colorado Blue Spruce

Rodeo

DE

on 12/7/1787 it became the 1st state

Delaware
Dover

"Liberty and Independence"

The First State

American Holly

Strawberry

Horseshoe Crab

Tiger Swallowtail

Blue Hen Chicken

Lady Bug

Peach Blossom

FL

Florida
Tallahassee

on 3/3/1845 it became the 27th state

"In God We Trust"

The Sunshine State

- Sabal Palm
- Alligator
- Orange Blossom
- Panther
- Cape Canaveral
- Disney World
- Manatee
- Mockingbird

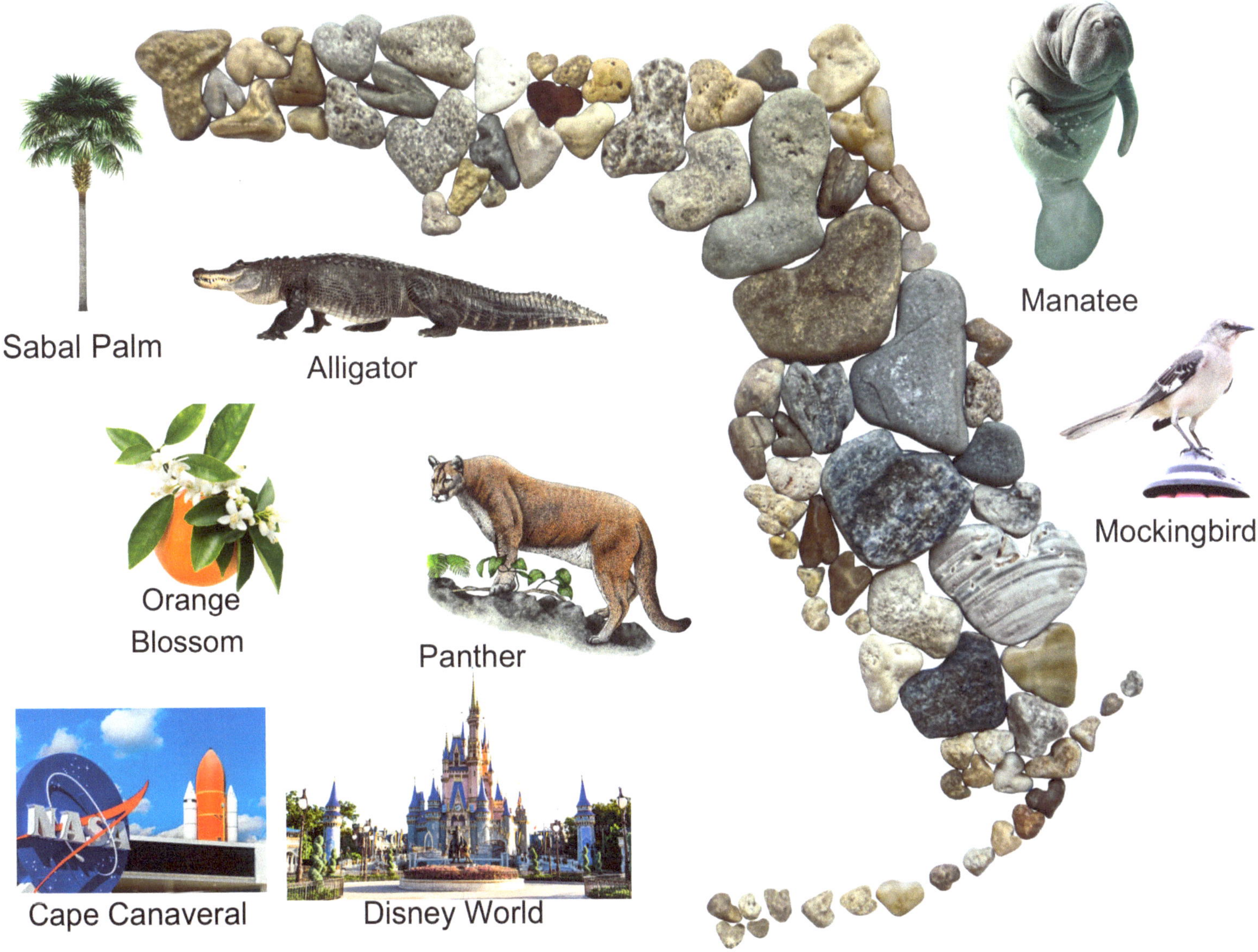

GA

Georgia
Atlanta

on 3/3/1845 it became the 27th state
"Wisdom, Justice, Moderation"
The Peach State

Southern Live Oak

Cherokee Rose

Large Mouth Bass

Brown Thrasher

Peanuts

Peaches

HI

Hawaii

Honolulu

on 8/20/1959 it became the 50th state

"The Life of the Land is Perpetuated in Righteousness"

The Aloha State

Nene-Branta Sandvicensis

Candlenut

Pua Aloalo

Surfing

Humpback Whale

Coffee

Kilauea Volcano

ID
Idaho
Boise

on 7/3/1890 it became the 43rd state

"Esto Perpetua" (let it be perpetual)

The Gem State

Mountain Bluebird

Western White Pine

Potatoes

Syringar

IL   on 12/3/1818 it became the 21st state

"State, Sovereignty, National Union"

The Prairie State

Illinois

Springfield

White Oak

Violet

Mountain Bluebird

Aurora City of Lights

World's Fair 1893

Indiana

Indianapolis

on 12/11/1816 it became the 19th state

"The Crossroads of America"

The Hoosiers State

Tulip

Peony

Cardinal

Indianapolis 500

IA  on 12/28/1846 it became the 29th state

Iowa

Des Moines

"Our Liberties We Prize And Our Rights We Will Maintain"

The Hawkeye State

Bur Oak

Eastern Goldfinch

Wild Prairie Rose

KS

Kansas
Topeka

on 1/29/1861 it became the 34th state

"Ad Astra Per Aspera"
(to the stars through difficulty)
The Sunflower State

Western Meadowlark

Wild Sunflower

Eastern Cottonwood tree

LA

Louisiana

Baton Rouge ⭐

on 4/30/1812 it became the 18th state

"Union, Justice and Confidence"

The Pelican State

Eastern Brown Pelican

Bald Cypress

New Orleans
Mardi Gras

Magnolia flower

ME

Maine
Augusta

on 3/15/1820 it became the 23rd state
"I Direct"
The Pine Tree State

Wild Blueberries

White Pine Cone and Tassel Flower

Chickadee

Lobster

White Pine

MD Maryland Annapolis

on 4/28/1788 it became the 7th state

"Strong Deeds, Gentle Words"

The Old Line State

Baltimore Oriole

Black Eyed Susan

White Oak

MA

Massachusetts
★ Boston

on 2/6/1788 it became the 6th state

"By the sword we seek peace, but peace only under liberty"

The Bay State

Trailing Arbatus

Chickadee

American Elm

Pilgrims and 1st Thanksgiving

Boston Tea Party

MN

on 1/26/1837 it became the 26th state

Minnesota

"The Star of the North"
The North Star State

Saint Paul

Red Pine

Common Loon

Ladyslipper

MS
Mississippi
Jackson

on 12/10/1817 it became the 20th state

"Be Valor and Arms"
The Magnolia State

Southern Magnolia

Mockingbird

Magnolia

MO

on 8/10/1821 it became the 24th state

"The Welfare of the People
is the Highest Law"

The Show Me State

Missouri

Jefferson City

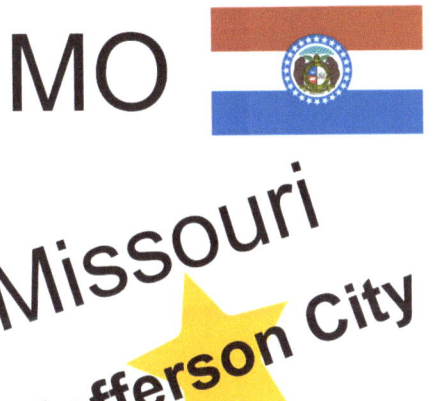

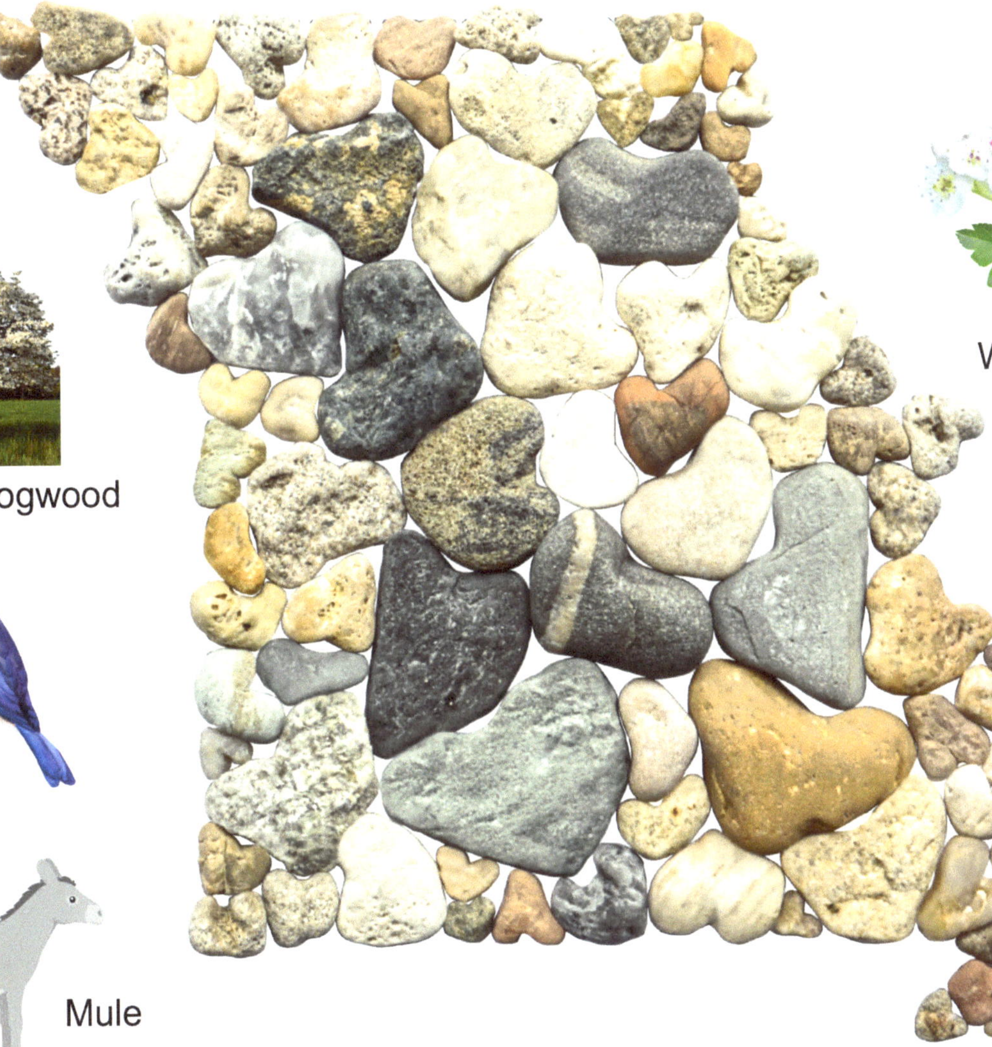

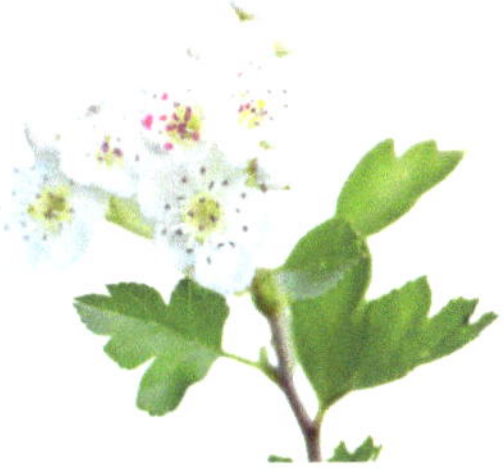

White Hawthorn
Blossom

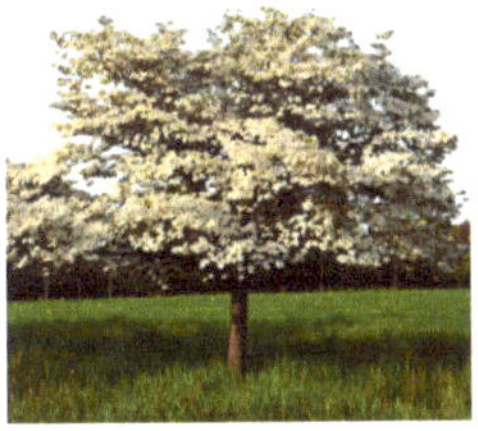

Flowering Dogwood

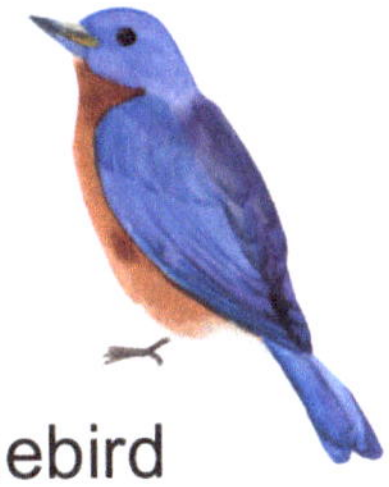

Bluebird

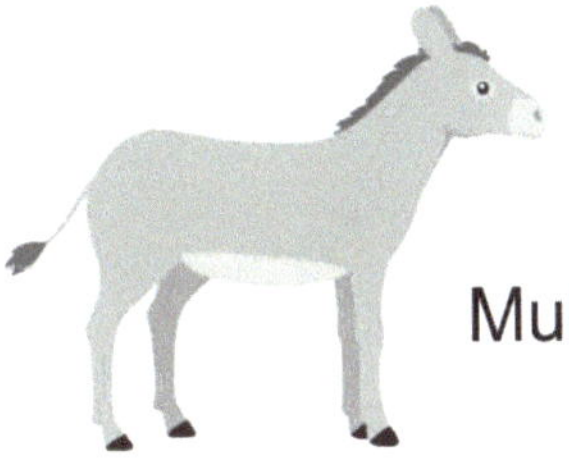

Mule

MT  on 11/8/1889 it became the 41st state
"Gold and Silver"
The Treasure State

Montana

★ Helena

Ponderosa Pine

Western Meadowlark

Grizzly Bear

Bitterroot Flower

NE  on 3/1/1864 it became the 36th state

"Equity Before Law"

The Cornhusker State

Nebraska

Lincoln ★

- Eastern Cottonwood
- Western Meadowlark 
- Honeybee 
- Goldenrod

NV

Nevada

Carson City ★

on 3/1/1864 it became the 36th state

"All for Our Country"

The Silver State

Single Leaf Pinyon Pine

Sagebrush flower

Bluebird

WELCOME TO Fabulous LAS VEGAS NEVADA

Hoover Dam

NH

on 6/21/1788 it became the 9th state

"Live Free or Die"

The Granite State

New Hampshire

⭐ **Concord**

Purple Lilac

Paper Birch

Mount Washington

Purple Finch

NJ

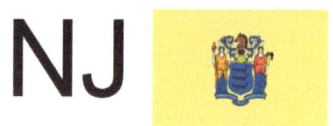

on 12/18/1787 it became the 3rd state

"Liberty and Prosperity"

The Garden State

New Jersey

Trenton

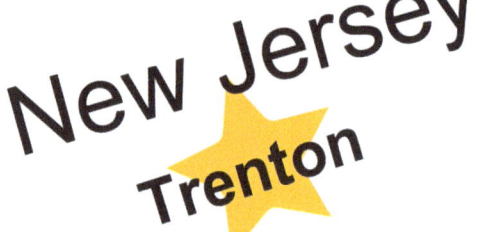

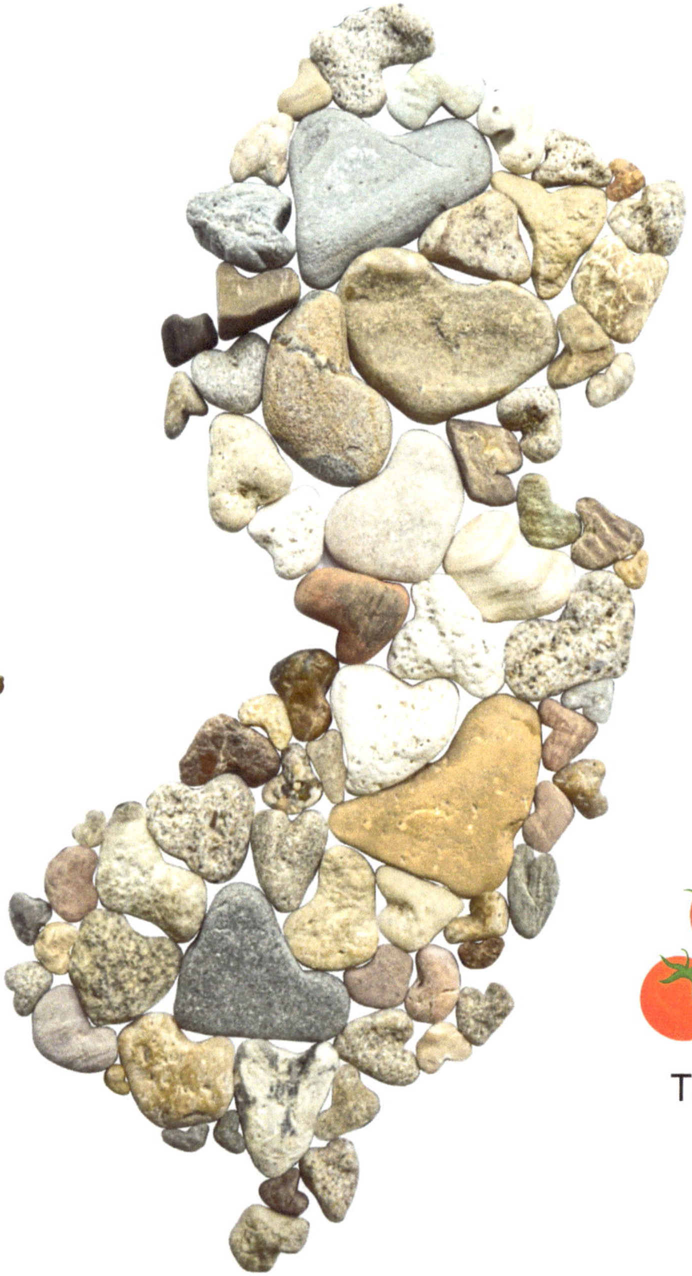

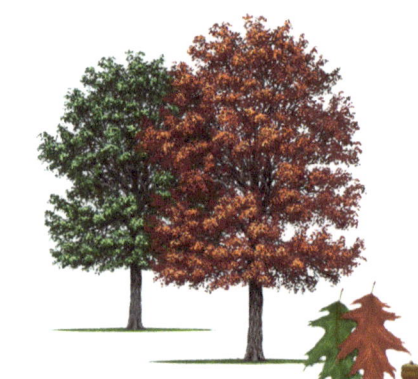

Northern Red Oak

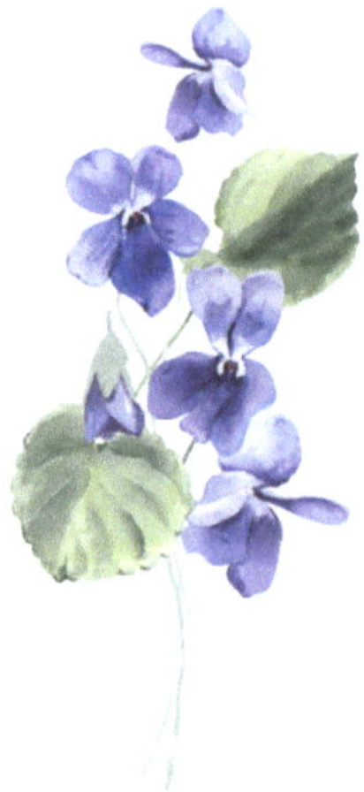

Violet

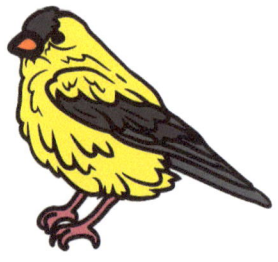

Goldfinch

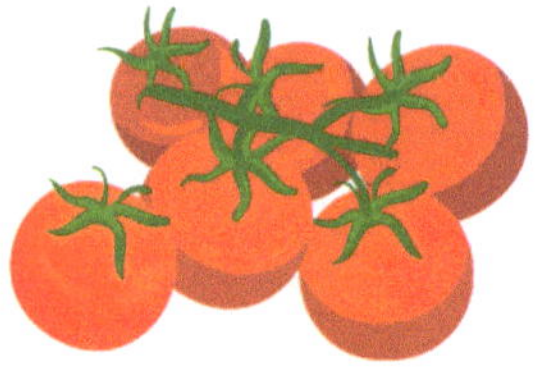

Tomatoes

NM  on 1/6/1912 it became the 47th state

New Mexico
"It Grows as it Goes"
Land of Enchantment

Santa Fe

Roadrunner

Yucca

Piñon Tree

NC  on 11/21/1789 it became the 12th state

"To be rather than to seem (to be)"

Tar Heel State

North Carolina
Raleigh

Dogwood flower

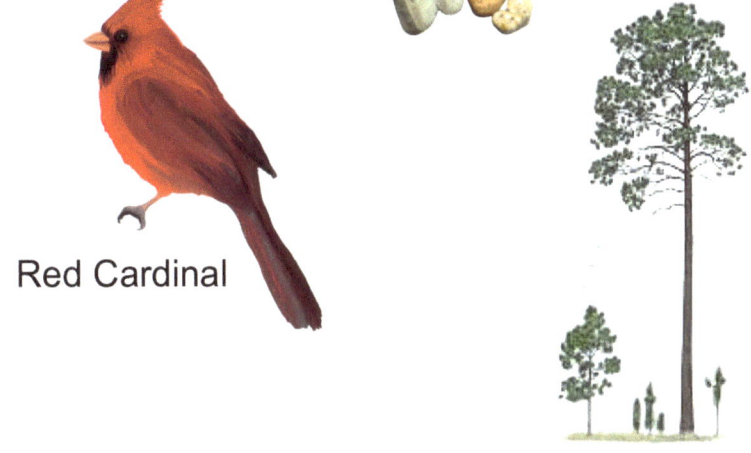
Red Cardinal

Longleaf Pine

Outer Banks

ND

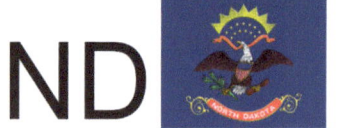

on 11/2/1889 it became the 39th state

"Liberty and Union
One and Inseperable"

The Peace Garden State

North Dakota

Bismarck

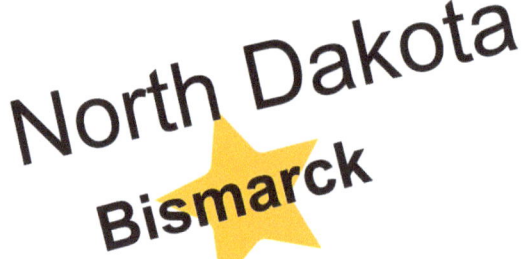

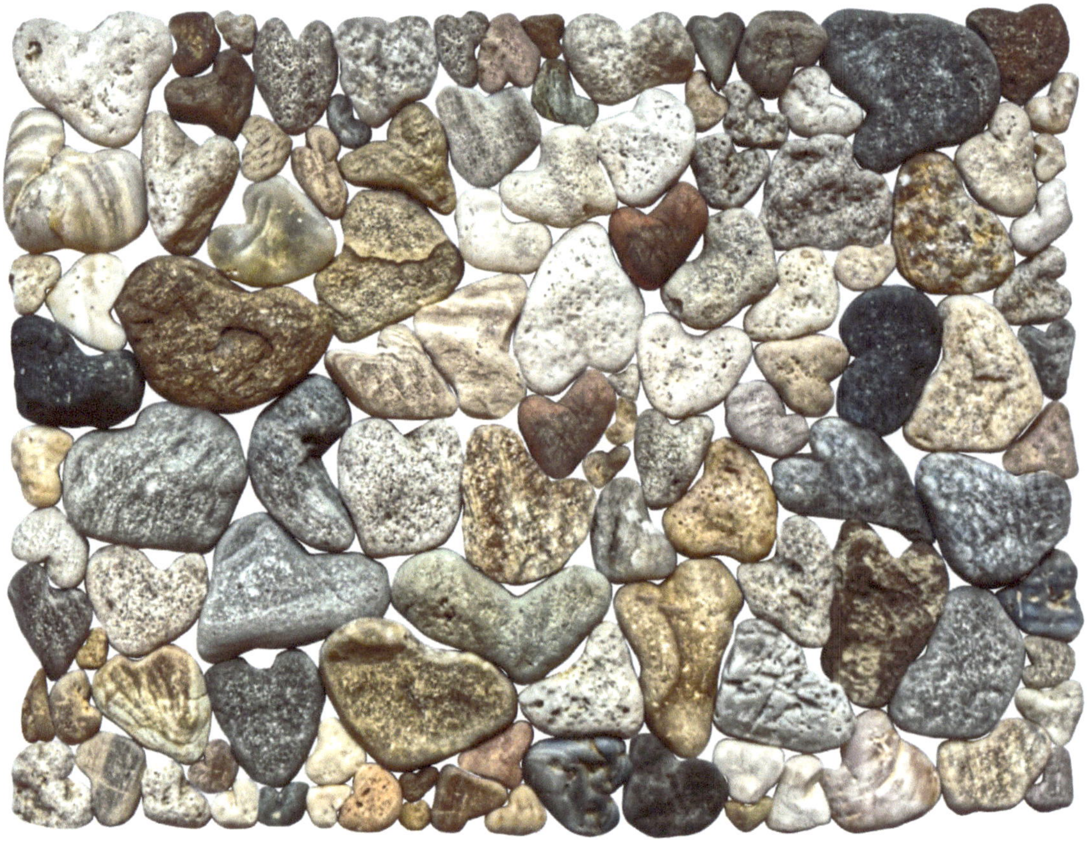

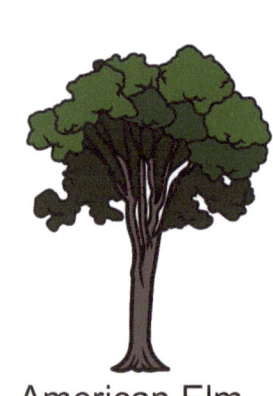

American Elm

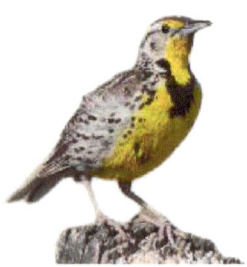

Western Meadowlark

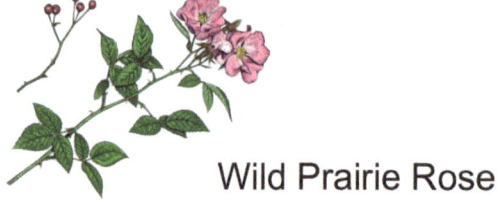

Wild Prairie Rose

OK  on 11/16/1907 it became the 46th state

"Hard Work Conquers All Things"

The Sooner State

Oklahoma

Oklahoma City

Eastern Redwood

Rose

Scissor Tailed Flycatcher

OR

Oregon

⭐ Salem

on 2/14/1859 it became the 33rd state

"She Flies With Her Own Wings"

The Beaver State

Douglas Fir

Oregon Grape

Western Meadowlark

Hazelnuts

PA  on 12/12/1787 it became the 2nd state

"Virtue, Liberty and Independence"

The Keystone State

Pennsylvania

Salem ★

Eastern Hemlock

Ruffed Grouse

Puxatawney Philo

Mountain Laurel

RI  on 5/29/1790 it became the 13th state

"Hope"

The Ocean State

Rhode Island
Providence

Rhode Island Red Hen

Watch Hill Flying Horse Carousel

Red Maple

Block Island

Newport Mansions

SD

South Dakota
Pierre

on 11/2/1889 it became the 40th state

"Under God People Rule"

The Mount Rushmore State

White Spruce

Americana Pasque flower

Ring Necked Pheasant

Mount Rushmore

on 6/1/1796 it became the 16th state

"Agriculture and Commerce"

The Volunteer State

Tennessee

Nashville

Mockingbird

Iris

Tulip Tree

Country Music

TX

on 12/29/1845 it became the 28th state
"Friendship"
The Lone Star State

Texas
★ Austin

Armadillo

Mockingbird

Bluebonnet Flower

Pecan Tree

UT

on 1/4/1896 it became the 45th state

"Industry"

The Beehive State

Utah — Salt Lake City

Sego Lily

Quaking Aspen

Rainbow Trout

Ring Billed Gull

VT  Vermont

on 3/4/1791 it became the 14th state

"Freedom & Unity and May the 14th Star Shine Bright"

The Green Mountain State

Montpelier ★

Mountains

Red Clover

Sugar Maple

Maple Syrup

Hermit Thrush-Catharus

Skiing

VA  on 6/26/1788 it became the 10th state
"Thus Always to Tyrants"
The Old Dominion State

Virginia ⭐ **Richmond**

Dogwood Blossom

Flowering Dogwood

Cardinal Grosbeak

Beaches

WA  on 11/11/1889 it became the 42nd state

Washington

"Bye and Bye"

The Evergreen State

Olympia ⭐

Willow Goldfinch

Apples

Coast Rhododendron

Western Hemlock

Glaciers

WI   on 5/29/1848 it became the 30th state

"Forward"

The Badger State

Wisconsin

Madison

Violet

Sugar Maple

American Robin

WY

Wyoming
Cheyenne

on 5/29/1848 it became the 30th state

"Equal Rights"
The Equality State

Old Faithful Geyser

Yellowstone Park

Plains Cottonwood

Paintbrush Flower

Western Meadowlark

Dedicated to my family and friends. Thank you for your love and support during my life. You all inspire me to keep moving forward.

David, my amazing husband, I love you completely. You are my North Star. I am so grateful for you. You are my beloved and my soul mate. Thank you for loving me.

Sean, Dillon and Austin, you are my world. No words could ever express how much I love you. I am so proud of you and being your mom has been my greatest gift. Jackson and Drew, you have brought so much joy into my life. I love you.
Mom, you've been my biggest fan, biggest cheerleader. Thank you for your love, support and wisdom. I love you.

Stay in the moment and follow your heart.

www.ingramcontent.com/pod-product-compliance
Lightning Source LLC
Chambersburg PA
CBHW042010090426
42811CB00015B/1608